Pebble® Plus

Animal Communication

by Abbie Dunne

CAPSTONE PRESS
a capstone imprint

Pebble Plus is published by Capstone Press,
1710 Roe Crest Drive, North Mankato, Minnesota 56003
www.mycapstone.com

Library of Congress Cataloging-in-Publication Data
Names: Dunne, Abbie, author.
Title: Animal communication / by Abbie Dunne.
Description: North Mankato, Minnesota : Capstone Press, [2017] | Series:
   Pebble plus. Life science | Audience: Ages 4-8.? | Audience: K to grade
   3.? | Includes bibliographical references and index.
Identifiers: LCCN 2016005324| ISBN 9781515709435 (library binding) | ISBN
   9781515709756 (pbk.) | ISBN 9781515711100 (ebook pdf)
Subjects: LCSH: Animal communication--Juvenile literature. | Animal
   behavior--Juvenile literature.
Classification: LCC QL751.5 .D87 2017 | DDC 591.59--dc23
LC record available at http://lccn.loc.gov/2016005324

Editorial Credits
Linda Staniford, editor; Bobbie Nuytten, designer; Jo Miller, media researcher;
Tori Abraham, production specialist

Photo Credits
Minden Pictures: Kim Taylor, 5; Science Source: E. R. Degginger, 19; Shutterstock: Chones, 20, Eric Gevaert, 11,
MarcusVDT, 21, Olga Visavi, 17, Paul Reeves Photography, 1, 7, Rejja, 13, Rob Hainer, cover, steve estvanik, 15;
Thinkstock: Jupiterimages/PHOTOS.com, 9

Design Elements
Shutterstock: Alena P

Note to Parents and Teachers

The Life Science set supports national curriculum standards for science. This book introduces
the concept of animal communication. The images support early readers in understanding the
text. The repetition of words and phrases helps early readers in understanding the text. This
book also introduces early readers to subject-specific vocabulary words, which are defined in
the Glossary section. Early readers may need assistance to read some words and to use the
Table of Contents, Glossary, Read More, Internet Sites, Critical Thinking Using the Common
Core, and Index sections of the book.

Printed and bound in China.
007691

Table of Contents

How Do Animals Communicate?

Animals can't talk.

But they do communicate.

Whales sing underwater.

Bees dance to tell other bees

where to find food.

Sound

Birds sing to send messages to other birds. One song may mean, "Come build a nest with me." Another song may signal danger.

Smell

Smell tells animals many things. It tells them whether to come or go. A moth's scent attracts other moths. A skunk's stinky spray says, "Stay away!"

Body Language

Animals use their bodies to communicate too. Nervous chimpanzees show their teeth. Gorillas frown when they are worried.

Sometimes dogs wag their tails
to say they are happy. When dogs
want to play, they lower their
upper bodies to the ground.

Touch

A touch can say many things.
Elephants show love by
touching trunks. Cats rub
their owner's leg when they
want attention.

Colors and Lights

Octopuses communicate

by changing their skin color.

The colors are signals

to other octopuses.

Some animals communicate with light. Fireflies glow in the darkness. The flashes of light send messages to other fireflies.

Activity

How do honeybees tell each other where to find nectar? Find out!

What You Need

- group of friends or family
- packets of sugar or sugar cubes
- floor space

What You Do

1. Name one person the scout bee. Everyone else is a worker bee.

2. Have everyone but the scout bee leave the room. Ask the scout bee to hide the sugar.

3. Have the scout bee make up a dance. The dance should tell the worker bees where to find the sugar.

4. Ask everyone to come back into the room. Then have the scout bee perform the dance.

5. Ask the worker bees to find the sugar. Did any bees find it?

6. Choose a new scout bee and repeat steps 2–5.

What Do You Think?

Make a claim.

A claim is something you believe to be true.

How do honeybees tell other bees where to find food?

Glossary

attention—playing, talking, and being with someone or something

attract—to get the attention of someone or something

communicate—share information, thoughts, or feelings

message—facts, ideas or feelings sent to someone or something

nervous—uneasy or worried

scent—a smell

signal—a message between our brains and our senses

underwater—under the surface of the water

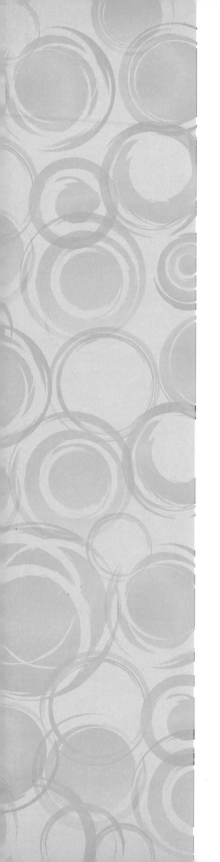

Read More

Davies, Nicola. *Talk, Talk, Squawk! A Human's Guide to Animal Communication*. Somerville, Mass.: Candlewick Press, 2011.

Townsend, John. *Amazing Animal Communicators*. Animal Superpowers. Chicago: Raintree, 2013.

Yaw, Valerie. *Color-Changing Animals*. Animals with Super Powers. New York: Bearport Publishing, 2011.

Internet Sites

FactHound offers a safe, fun way to find Internet sites related to this book. All of the sites on FactHound have been researched by our staff.

Here's all you do:

Visit *www.facthound.com*

Type in this code: 9781515709435

 Check out projects, games and lots more at
www.capstonekids.com

Critical Thinking Using the Common Core

1. Explain what communication means. (Craft and Structure)

2. List three ways in which animals communicate. (Key Ideas and Details)

3. A skunk's spray smells terrible. What do you think this communicates to other animals? (Integration of Knowledge and Ideas)

4. Why do you think animals that live in dark places use lights to communicate with each other? (Integration of Knowledge and Ideas)

Index